D0292594

My Kid Is an Asshole,

and So Is My Dog

Bestselling Author

Diana Stefano

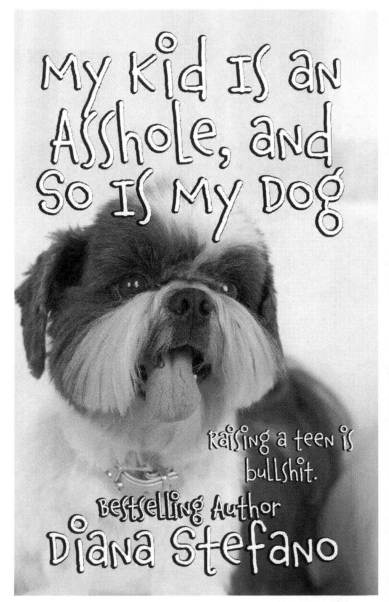

My Kid Is an Asshole, and So Is My Dog

raising a teen is bullshit.

Bestselling Author Diana Stefano

My Kid Is an Asshole, and So Is My Dog

Crazy Ink
www.crazyink.org
My Kid Is an Asshole, and So Is My Dog/Stefano.—
1st ed.

My Kid Is an Asshole, and So Is My Dog

For Stephen, Savanna, Shane and Kaitlyn
Maybe Karl & Cletus, too

Thanks for giving me a life full of love, laughter,
chaos and making every day an adventure. Oh, and
thanks for the material for this book. I think.

I love you guys.

This is a humor book.

If you don't have a sense of humor, do not read this book.

I repeat, if you do not have a sense of humor, do not read this book.

If colorful language bothers you, do not read this book.

If you are looking for actual parenting advice:

Get your tubes tied.

Yes, I said it, and I know you want to, too.

My kid is an asshole. No, I'm serious. Put the book down right now if you don't like cussing, because it's about to be thrown at you like a monkey throwing shit when it's mad. You've been forewarned. But, then again, the title should have given it away.

I just had a conversation with my 15-year-old daughter. Basically, it's about her grades. She doesn't like it when I harp on her. I don't like it when her grades suck, so you can imagine how those conversations go. But this one. Yes, this one. It's a gem. I think I'll write it down and put it in her "special box" alongside her grade school art and achievements and pull it out when I need a reminder of why I'm so fucking thankful I had a hysterectomy four years ago. I simply informed her, very matter-of-fact, that she could not get her driver's license until all of her grades were passing. Her response?

"Okay, well, after the time where I could have got my license, and I should be driving, then you can't complain anymore about having to drive me around since I should be driving myself."

Wait. What? I can't complain because you should have your driver's license but don't have it because you're not getting with the program? Um, okay. Challenge accepted, sister. Listen up, Princess, not only will I complain (if I ever even let you back in the car), but I will also remind you at every red light why you're not driving on your own, and I will, yes I will, subject you to Neil Diamond's greatest hits while I sing along loud and proud with the sunroof open and windows down. Thirty degrees out? Don't care. Bring a jacket. Maybe a scarf. Friends watching? Hmmm. I've always loved an audience. Bring it.

She wasn't always like this. No, she wasn't always condescending or stubborn and she didn't always have to have it her way. After all, she has probably heard the phrase, "This isn't Burger King, you don't get it your way," more times than she can count. She was sweet at one point. Loving. She cuddled. She wanted me to watch her when she did something cool. She wore leggings and silk-screened t-shirts that I picked out. And she loved them, or at least she pretended she did. She sang to me. She read to me. She did well in school. She was an athlete.

Then somewhere along the line, she just became an asshole. It was like as soon as she realized the tooth fairy wasn't real, she got a dose of the hormone fairy which WAS real and let me tell you— the hormone fairy is an asshole, too. I wonder if I leave a dollar under her pillow when she's PMSing if the fairy will wave a magic wand and make it go away, but I doubt it. I don't think there's a cure for this. She's the long-awaited karma my mother wished on me when I was sixteen. Well played, Mom. Well played. PS: I'm sending her to live with you for the summer. And she's bringing the damn dogs.

Speaking of dogs, I can't count how many times I've had to pick up the trash after they've tipped it over. And I swear, I can't even have people over anymore because, did you know, Shih Tzus can jump? Not only can they jump, but they can head butt you too. I'm just not sure I have enough homeowner's insurance to handle the claims anymore.

I'm surrounded by assholes. Big ones, little ones, girl ones, boy ones, furry ones. You get the picture.

Now, before you all have a collective heart attack about what an asshole *I am,* I will admit that I was "that" teenager too. So, she comes by it naturally. It's hereditary, I think. Although, I had another daughter who wasn't quite this assholic. So, I can pride myself there. Maybe because she was the first born. Maybe it skips a "generation." Fuck, I

9

don't know. But what I know now is my mini-me is a terrorist. A full-blown terrorist.

And, just a caveat, I don't really have the answers here. If you're looking for a solution to this problem, you might want to go pick up a book by somebody with a PhD or some shit. Because that's not me. All I can do is share my story and hope that if it hits home with you, you know you're not alone. All the Pinterest moms can suck it. I am too busy making sure my kid gets her shit together and lives a productive life to sew together all her old t-shirts in a heart on a quilt to remind her of the good old days that will just end up on a heap on her floor anyway. The closest I come to shit like that is slapping a pretzel stick in a peanut butter cup on Halloween and calling it a witch's broom. Okay, I *might* make her meatloaf on October 31st that looks like a rat, too. See, I am a good mom.

Seriously, though. I thought my experience as a horrible teenager would lend me a hand when I had to deal with my own. I was wrong. This is a whole new breed. It's like the young vampires in "Twilight." They're stronger. They're faster. They're mouthier. They have social media to contend with. The schools give them way too many breaks. They have too many choices. They are treated with kid gloves way too much. Dr. Spock is an asshole too, by the way. My generation learned from him that parents shouldn't step on our itty-bitty toes. Well, guess what? We've produced a new generation of monsters. Run. Run fast. Get out while you can. Some people are worried about the zombie apocalypse. I'm worried about the teenager apocalypse. She's eating my brain. And my wallet.

By the way, did I mention the dogs? Have you ever heard a Shih Tzu bark? I have. Over and over. They think they're coyotes. I swear. And right now, they're wrestling over some stuffed animal, which is surely about to be flung open, so I can pick up little beads all over the carpet. No wait. They stopped. One of them had to drag their ass across the floor.

Oh good, now my roommate just came home and noticed the guacamole that is sitting on the counter. His first question?

"Who left the guacamole out?"

Oh, for fuck's sake. Like you don't already know.

"The terrorist."

Why even ask? No, I did not come home and dig through the guacamole and leave it out with the top off so that it now looks like the diarrhea of a newborn. Hey, let's invite some friends over later. There's still some left. Just squirt some lemon in it and add some green food coloring and mix it around. It was like $5.99. We're using every last drop of that crap. But I really don't get it. Is there a reason she couldn't have put it away before she left? Was the house on fire? Did a meteor hit the field down the street? Maybe she was kidnapped and couldn't help it? Yeah, no. I have her on "find my friends" on my phone. She's fine. At her friend's, likely telling them how horrible I am. Hey, maybe if she can pay

12

attention in English for a millisecond, she can learn to write and start her own book. You know, the sequel to this one; *"My Mom is an Asshole."*

I just got an email from her speech teacher. Apparently, she's behind two speeches and one paper. Ok, so, 1. Her speeches are written and would take like 2 minutes to present and, 2. The paper she's missing? It's in her binder. IN HER BACKPACK. The same one I see her taking to school every day. What in the actual fuck? Is it too hard to take the paper out, that's completely done and done correctly (because I watched her do it) and turn it in? Do I have to write her a note?

Dear mini me,

When you get to speech class, open your backpack and remove your binder. Take out the completed paper entitled, "Passive vs Active Listening." Hand it to your teacher.

xoxo,

Your birth mother

She would probably lose the note. Maybe I will have to text it to her. Oh wait, I have. Like seriously, it's that hard? I wish I had another kid that went to school with her, but no. They had to grow up. They left. I'm sure you aren't wondering why, ha-ha. But, with one in the military and one in college, there's nobody left to help. At least when my son went through this phase he had to pay his sister $2.00 to deliver his papers to his teachers. If he couldn't do it, then she would. For a price. That lasted about two weeks until he was tired of being broke.

But, really, why can't they turn in their work? Do they forget? Mini-stroke? Alien abduction?

Anyway, I told the teacher that, but then suggested that maybe I would have to deliver the paper myself and charge the kid a delivery fee. The teacher suggested that if it worked, I could buy myself a drink. So, I challenged her. I told her that if she could get the kid to turn in her paper and give her speeches, I would buy the teacher a drink. Game on. I'm okay with bribes.

Maybe I should go to school with her. Are scrunchies still in fashion? Big hair? Hoop earrings? Neon? Jelly shoes? I could make braces out of tin foil and fit right in. Maybe I could take one of the dogs as an emotional support animal, but I'm pretty sure we would get kicked out when somebody tried to pick the fucker up and it turned into a gremlin-looking growling thing. Have you ever seen a Shih Tzu growl? Oh please, go pick one up that doesn't want to be picked up. You'll laugh. You need that. Just don't get your face bit off. That would be gross. Go on. I'll wait.

If you still have your face and arms and legs intact, I'm wondering if this going to school and embarrassing thing works. Like, am I alone in this idea? I asked a friend. You know. Just to get some suggestions. Bad idea?

Hell no. Because after her kid was an asshole and then demanded she "wear something cute and not embarrass her" at the award ceremony the next day, my hero mom friend showed up in a Chewbacca mask and roared and clapped with her little miss looking on in pure disgust. As mom said it, "Gauntlet dropped!" Yaaaaaaas. I either have some really screwed up friends or they're brilliant. I choose genius!

My Kid Is an Asshole, and So Is My Dog

Sorry, your kid is an Asshole, too.

I always have to laugh when people don't think their kids are assholes, too. All kids are assholes. I hate to break it to you, but your kid is an asshole. In fact, I used to have a friend who thought her kids were perfect and if we were still friends, I would tell her that her kids are assholes as well.

How do you know? What kind of asshole is your kid?

Well, let's break it down. Hammer-time.

1.   The Eddie Haskell:

I know, I'm dating myself here. But if you're my age, you know who Eddie Haskell is. If you're too young to know who he is, then you're too young to have a teenager. Unless, of course, you're reading this to prepare yourself for one. That's not a bad idea. Preemptive strikes work. Anyway, who (my age) can forget Eddie Haskell from "Leave it to Beaver," you know—that all American teenager who was so polite and respectful to parents and then a creep behind their backs? They still exist. It might be your kid. If everybody is always telling you how wonderful your kid is but he's always in trouble and it's always because he's in the "wrong place at the wrong time with the wrong kids," then it's probably your kid that's the problem. Accept it.

2. The Brooder:

The kid that never smiles. Everything is always wrong. They don't always wear black, but they never change the look on their face. They sound like Eeyore when they talk and "I can't" and "It won't" is part of their everyday vocabulary. Every day is a pity party, yet if you actually threw one, they wouldn't show up because you know, it would suck.

3.   The Drama Queen:

Yes, we all know this one. And it's not just girls who fit this bill. It's the kid who finds the drama in EVERYTHING, not just the negative. In fact, it can be kinda funny sometimes. My mom nicknamed me "Sarah Bernhardt," who I guess was some huge dramatic actress in the late 1800's/early 1900's. I don't know why. Throwing myself on the floor and writhing around complaining about something was not an act. If I were going to flop around the floor like a dead fish, you can bet your ass it was for good reason.

4.   The Cry Baby:

19

I just can't. If your kid is a crier and over the age of ten, just leave them at home. All of us parents understand that sometimes, kids cry. Sometimes, there's a really good reason too. But if they cry at the drop of the hat because their feelings were hurt, just keep them home. Please. We want to enjoy your kid. We want to take them to the movies and the mall and out to dinner. But we do not want to have to deal with a kid that can't, at times, either roll with the joke or they turn into #2 because something rubbed them the wrong way. Tell them to get over it, help if they need it - or just don't let them out of the house. For real. On the flip side, we don't want any Pollyanna crap, either. Life is not rainbows and unicorns; we do not need fairy dust shoved up our ass. Find balance, people! Quick!

5.   The Goodie-Two-Shoes:

Listen up. No one likes this kind of kid. This kid is also referred to as the "party pooper" and the "buzz kill." While we like the kid that behaves and listens and follows the rules, we do not like the kid who judges us and our kids as they do it. I have a friend whose own daughter wouldn't sneak into a movie with her no matter how many times she convinced her that it was okay because the movie was about over, they had already dropped a cool hundred in snacks, and the movie attendant was a classic #1 and didn't give a shit if they popped in there. No. She made them walk out of the movie theater, buy a new ticket, and go in. Her grandma said that was okay, so that it was off her conscience. Okay. Fine. I'm glad she can sleep at night. Trust me, we want our kids to sleep at night. But, hot damn – live a little.

6.   The Nellie Oleson:

Okay, another character you might have to look up, so go ahead and grab your Google. But for the love of all that is Holy, please don't raise one of these. The tattling. The smirking. The passive-aggressive bully. Please. Do us all a favor and do what I do. Tell your kids if they're not "dead, dying, or bleeding" to save it.

7.   The kid that's never moving out of your house:

Okay, look, I don't have empty nest syndrome. Maybe you do, I don't know. But if you are raising a combo of #2, #3 & #4, they're never leaving and it will be your fault. They're going to play video games all night, sleep all day, and complain about everything.

They're going to live on chips and Mountain Dew and have no human interaction. Then one day, you're going to die and they're going to have to be moved to a mental institution because they not only won't have any of their own kids to torture and move in with, but they're not going to know how to hold a conversation or hold down a job and it's going to be your fault. Just sayin'.

8.   The Over-Achiever:

Not too dissimilar from #5, but the thing that is bad about this one is the stress these kids put on themselves. I mean, we're all for doing the best you can, but it's also okay to take a break sometimes. I have one of these and I'm proud as all get out of her, but I also don't want her to get so lost in overdoing it that she forgets to relax.

9.   The Comedian:

I have one of these, too. And he's so funny. But he drove me nuts when he was a teenager. I started posting everything he said on social media in an effort to get him to shut up, but it just made it worse. His "Shane-isms" brought roars of laughter. He loved the attention. Now, as a grown-up, he doesn't anymore. He actually makes me ask for permission to post the things he says. Because he's still fucking hilarious. But I am so thankful that I didn't believe the things he said, because I might have had to have him evaluated or my blood pressure checked.

10.   The All-Around Asshole:

This one takes the cake. Literally. They come into your house, exhibit all the characteristics of #1-9, and they eat all your food. There are some of my kids' friends who can come live here permanently. There are some who can come in and sit on the couch and put their feet up. But the kid I don't know who starts rifling through my fridge and my pantry can get out. Pronto. You have to earn that shit. That is a right given only to a few. Go eat at home. This is not McDonalds and I am not a short order cook. And why is all of your stuff in my guest room? Did you move in? You're evicted. Out.

Does any of that sound remotely familiar? Because if it does, your kid is an asshole too. It might be one thing or a combination of several, but I know you can identify with some of it. If you can't, then you're the parent of the year. Go celebrate. Just not at my house. All my cake is gone. Your kid ate it.

3%

I honestly feel like we all need to take cover right now. Like, I'm seriously looking for a place to hide. I am getting ready to ask a friend to cover me while I move the dogs out one by one for their safety, but, oh my God, probably one of the worst things that could go wrong is happening. Right now. She's lost her phone charger.

"Charger" is a four-letter word around here, and a word that will inevitably start a remake of the Trojan War. I'm pretty sure if she doesn't find it soon, she's gonna channel her inner "Xena – Warrior Princess" and charge through the house with her sword held high and a battle cry in her voice because the minute you say "charger" around this house, all hell breaks loose. I'm not kidding; that one time, when she was at 3%, I'm pretty sure she fucking spun her head around and threw up on the walls. I was surprised she didn't go into convulsions, but there

26

was this really subtle shaking in her hands and I just knew at any minute she was going to lose it. Thank God I had an extra charger because, I swear, if she had to look for one for two more minutes, she was going to make a tin foil hat and stick her hand in a socket to charge the damn thing herself. So, yeah, we avoid that conversation as much as possible.

So, this. This is not good. *No, this is not good.*

It's about this time that she would normally steal the charger off my nightstand, but since I am sitting in the living room, she can't get past me and in my room without me seeing and asking her what she's doing. It's quiet up in her room; I'm guessing because her phone is dead, and she can't play her music off of it. Thank God for that. It's shitty music anyway, but the sound of silence is scary. Like, really scary.

The silence reminds me of another time when she stole my charger. I demanded she bring it back, and she did, but between the time that I asked her and the time she made it to my room, there was this eerie silence as we waited for her to appear. Total quiet. Until we heard the stomping. First down the stairs, then across the carpet in the living room, then across the wood floor in the hall. Bam, bam, bam, bam, bam. The blood rushed through my veins, causing my heart to pound waiting for the door to be flung open. At that moment, I was hoping it was her because, if it wasn't, from the sound of things, it was Godzilla. Not sure which one would have been better at that moment. Fire breathing dragons or a fifteen-year-old.

But tonight, oh yes, tonight, it's silent again. The calm before the storm. I have to take action. I must get my war plan together. And pronto. I cannot let her sense weakness.

As I see it, I have two choices. Well, three, I guess, if I want to sacrifice my own phone access. I can:

1.   **Surrender my charger without a word.**

2.   **Confront her about where hers is and ask her why she doesn't have it, then follow up with a lecture on responsibility (because that's worked so well before),**

or

3.   **I can go buy her a new charger.**

Oh yes, I can hear it now. Every perfect parent out there is screaming silently, or even out loud, "DO NOT BUY HER A PHONE CHARGER." "TEACH HER RESPOSIBILITY." "DON'T LET HER GET AWAY WITH IT."

Alright, thank you to all the parents out there who have all the answers. I appreciate it. And, trust me, I've done it. I have taken her phone away. I have taken privileges away. I have made her go to bed at night without a charged phone, much like our parents made us go to bed without dinner. And guess what?

She doesn't give a fuck.

Just like we didn't care if our dinner was still sitting out at breakfast from the night before because our mom told us that if we didn't eat what she had made for dinner, then by God, we would eat it for breakfast the next day. That'll teach us. Oh, come on, how many of you really had stale meatloaf for breakfast when you woke up because Mommy Dearest was trying to prove a point? And how many of you lapped up your dinner the next time she made it and didn't feed it to the dog under the table? Okay, so maybe some of you did out of pure fear, but for the most part, it's a bullshit call to arms and an unnecessary stand-off. Nobody wins. Because really, nobody wants salmonella poisoning. Not you, and even your mom knows she doesn't want you to get sick from eating food that is no good anymore, because then she has to be up with you all night cleaning vomit out of your hair.

So, let's be reasonable. I don't want to fight with my kid. I don't want her to feel like she can't tell me when she's screwed up. Because people screw up. She does. I do. You do.

I had a friend over at the time. She knew what was going on. She could feel it in the air. She knew what was coming. And then she offered this piece of advice:

"You know, she really needs a charger that stays here all the time. One that never leaves the house. Then she can take her other one with her to her friends' houses."

Brilliant.

I called her down and said nothing other than that I was taking her to the store. She happily got into the car. We drove to the store. I picked out a charger. She asked what that was for because she had found hers when she was upstairs. I told her that was fine, but this one was her home charger and could never leave the house. I would even color it or put stickers on it or whatever I needed to do, but it could never leave the house, so she would always have one there. She smiled.

Holy shit, she smiled. The heavens opened up in the middle of Walgreens and the Hallelujah chorus played. Angels slowly descended with their harps of gold and all was right in the world.

We got home. She had dinner. She offered to let me meet the boy she likes. She did her laundry.

And now, the next morning, she came to wake me, so I could give her a ride to school, because, well, you know – she still doesn't have a driver's license. But, when she woke me up, she kissed me on the cheek.

You know how often that happens anymore?

Christmas, my birthday, and when her phone is charged.

I'll take it.

I have learned a valuable lesson about picking and choosing my battles today. We always say we're going to do it, but we never do it. For us, buying the charger was a solution to the problem. It was proactive. Until she loses this one, it's there for her if she forgets her charger at her friend's or in somebody's car. It's not a big deal anymore. She's not going to come home and freak out because she can't post a selfie because her phone is dead.

I don't regret it for one second, and I'm going to do it again.

Having a bad hair day? *Here, let me buy you a charger.*

Friends being jerks? *Here, let me buy you a charger.*

Got an F on that test and you feel bad about it? *Here, let me buy you a charger.*

Teacher called you out in class? *Here, let me buy you a charger.*

Obviously, I'm not going to buy her a charger every time something goes wrong, but I am going to help her find a solution, not just after something happens but before. I am going to give her the tools to be proactive and, while I know this is a temporary fix and sooner or later some new drama is going to come up, I'm going to enjoy this moment. I am going to enjoy this victory. I am going to revel in the battle I chose not to fight.

I'm going to sip my coffee and do the dishes and not complain once about the crusty cereal bowl she finally brought out of her room after a month.

No, friends. I am going to enjoy the high. Because, right now, everything is good. And these moments are few and far between with a teenager in the house. I'm taking advantage of it. Today, she is not an asshole. And I'm loving every single second.

The Seven Deadly Sins

For thousands of years, philosophical masters have tried to figure out where the "Seven Deadly Sins" came from and what exactly they mean. They've literally gone to the ends of the earth doing research into it and some even died not knowing the answer. Well, listen, I've figured it out. No, it wasn't the Greeks or the Romans or some Biblical character. It was a mom describing her teenagers. And here's why:

1. **Gluttony:** Have you ever watched a teenager eat? I mean, heck, if I had that kind of metabolism, I would probably pack it away, too, but man—I can make my kid a full meal, watch her engulf it, and then ask for more. I often watch in disbelief and, silently, ask myself how it's even possible. *Why do we even give them silverware? Napkins? Why even bother having cups when they*

35

can just drink out of the container? Do they breathe in between bites? Do they chew? Wait, yes, they chew. I can hear it. Sometimes I can see it. Do they ever get full? Where does it go? I feel sorry for their digestive system, honestly. I feel sorry for my plumber. I feel sorry for the guy who is trying to decipher their special order at the fast food restaurant. And, why, for the love of all that's Holy, do they have to suck on their straw once all their drink is gone? Are they that hungry that they have to try to drink air? Is it the noise they like so much? Is it the fact that they just like to be irritating? I had two picky eaters and one not-so-much. She will eat anything. She licked an eyeball on a fish once. She tried escargot and swallowed it. I gagged. Who in their right mind actually *wants* to eat a snail? She knows how to make three things—

macaroni and cheese, eggs, and ramen noodles. Sometimes at different times, sometimes concurrently. I dread the day when she wants to cook for us, and we all have to try it. I see it now, "Scrambled eggs delicately laced with ramen noodles, topped with mac and cheese." And a side of toast. She can make that, too, which is evident by the crumbs she leaves behind. But really, how many boxes of cereal can a teenager eat at once? I used to tell my kids when they were little that if they ate their corn, they would be able to see it in their poop. If they ate their green vegetables, their poop would turn green. You know, creative ways to get them to eat, much like we put cheerios in the toilet for boys to pee on. But, I didn't know I was creating a monster. I didn't know that making eating fun when they were little would cause an astronomical grocery bill and multiple uses of the plunger. On top of that, teenagers can live on crap. If I have one too many spoons of ice cream, I am paying homage to the porcelain God for a month, yet they can live on Doritos and soda. Do they even take in any water? Does their body just know? Will they go into shock if they eat something healthy? What if there isn't any food in the house? Oh, that's okay. They memorize your credit card number and order $1500 worth of "Uber Eats" in a month. Did you know Uber delivers food? I didn't, until I got my credit card bill. There is actually an app you can order from and people who will show up at your door with a chocolate shake and a bag of fries at your request. If that doesn't scream lazy (see below – deadly sin #2), then I don't know what does. I thought for sure I was a victim of identity theft, and just when I was about to file a claim with the credit card company and all three reporting bureaus, I went through the itemized bill and saw that all the restaurants were local. I asked the terrorist about it and sure enough—she was hungry. Obviously famished, because she ordered enough food to feed a small village. I had to mentally write apology notes to all the phantom kids I cussed out in my head who I thought might have stolen my credit card and went on a binge-eating spree all over the country. I hope her ass gets fat.

2. **Sloth:** Mmmm, k. Really? Does this one even need an explanation? I wanted to get the correct definition of this so I could be very, very sure it related to teenagers. The definition reads, "(noun) reluctance to work or make an

effort, laziness." Ding, ding, ding. Now, you can't tell me that when somebody made up the seven deadly sins and decided to include laziness, they weren't talking about their own kid. I can hear the conversation somewhere in the sixth century. It goes like this:

"Lo, you there, child." A mother yells out to her teenager.

"Whaaaaaaaaat? Why thou callest me while I am sleeping?" He answers.

"Fetch me a water pail, so that I may draw your father a bath."

"Eh, he can do it himself. I'm tired."

"But, child, he works his hands to the bone for your comfort. He is weary and hungry upon his return. A hot bath will ease his tired body." The mother tries to reason.

"He'll get over it."

"Alright then, I shall do it myself."

"Mooooooooooom. Why you gotta be like that? Why you gotta make me feel guilty while I'm trying to sleep? Why don't you just ask?"

Oh, give me a break. Kids are lazy, they always have been, and we let them get away with it. Now, in saying that, I honestly have always thought that teenagers need more sleep than most people, so I always did try to let my kids sleep. But, like, fourteen hours a day? I wish I could do that. Not only can I not fall asleep very quickly, but I can't stay that way. If one thing or another doesn't hurt, it's the middle of the night bathroom visit that really wakes me up. How in the world do kids hold their bladder for that long anyway? Especially after all the crap they've ingested all day. Does Mountain Dew have like some kind of mystical power where they don't have to pee in the middle of their slumber? Is it hibernation? I watched a documentary on bears the other day and no shit, they can sleep for seven and a half months IN A ROW. Are our kids bears? Is this natural? Are they preparing for the winter? Zombies? I've found my kids sleeping everyplace. In beds, in closets, on the floor, in the kitchen, in chairs, in the car; everywhere. I seriously think this goes back to the fact that their body is mad at them for filling themselves up with crap and it puts them in a mini-coma to digest it all. But, yes, even I can get my kids to do chores. Lots of threats, bribery, crying, but, eventually, they help. One time, my daughter was so excited to show me how she cleaned up her room really nicely, and boy did she. It was beautiful. Everything in its place, cleaned out. Neatly arranged. Even some big things were missing, but that's okay, it gave her space. Until I found all her crap in the guest room the next week. I love parenting.

3. **Greed:** I'm not actually going to blame this one on teenagers. No, this starts when they're little assholic toddlers. That whiny, "It's mine" is only met with a whinier, "No, it's mine." Guess what, kids. It's MINE now. If you haven't uttered those words at some point, then you don't have multiple kids or you're not a real parent. So, we teach them. We teach them what's theirs and what isn't. We teach them how to share. We teach them how to give. We haul their ass to Goodwill to get rid of all our shit and give them this big long lecture about how we're giving things away to make somebody else's life better, and then we hold hands and sing kumbaya.

We all know that really, we're just trying to get rid of all the junk in our house and feel good about it, but it works most of the time when you want your kid to get rid of three hundred pounds of toys and you can't think of another way. At least when they're little and their hearts are still tender. "Listen, Johnny, there are kids in China who don't have half of what you do. Don't you think it would be nice to give them this stuffed animal? You know, the one you've had since you were two. The one with only one ear. Yes, dear. The one the dogs chewed the leg off of. I know, he was your special friend that week you had the chicken pox and he's probably totally contaminated but, yes, some little boy out there is going to love him just like you did. Probably even more because he is part of you." Yeah, that shit stops when they get older. They discover Craigslist and second-hand stores and gullible friends. They want to sell their stuff. Yes, the stuff you bought them. Do I get a commission here? Like, really? Remember that shirt I got you for Christmas that you said you loved and would wear every day? Why is Susie wearing it now? She's five times the size you are. I know her mother didn't buy her that. Are you getting it back? *"No, I sold it for five dollars."* Wait, hold up. You sold your $80 shirt that you never wore for $5.00? What the fuck for? Were you hungry? Will that even buy you a #1 anymore at McDonalds? With all the selling that goes on around here, I'm surprised she doesn't walk around with a credit card reader on her iPhone and have to pay taxes to the IRS. But, it's not like that money goes back to me. Oh, no. Greedy Gertrude hoards it for herself and

Manipulated Momma just buys her more when she needs it. Yep, totally guilty. I CAN'T HELP IT. I see the cutest outfit and I just have to get it because, well, I know how cute all her friends will look in it when she decides to open shop and go on a selling spree. And not only does she sell stuff to them, but she buys stuff from them. You think you're on top of your game when you sell some old shit on Facebook? No, let me tell you. You don't have anything on these kids. Nothing. They know exactly how to put together a "lot" of items, with one expensive piece and five crappy pieces and sell it for $50.00. And kids will pay! Well, their parents will pay. It's like the bundle of socks you get at the store. The ones on the outside are super cute and the three in the middle are plain Jane white. Same concept. Same scam. Next

Christmas, if I have any money left, she's getting a dog. The dogs are the only things we have that she doesn't want to get rid of, even when I want her to. And those are "all hers" too, until it's time to pick up poop. Then, they're not so greedy, are they?

4. **Lust:** Remember the hormone fairy? She's an asshole, too. One day, your sweet little girl is playing with her Barbies, setting them up for tea parties and getting them dressed for the school dance and the next, Barbie and Ken are making out in Barbie's dream camper. Suddenly, they've chopped off Barbie's golden locks and painted her nails and made her more appealing to Ken, or their brother's G.I. Joe. Aw, they're growing up. It's a fact of life. But, these girls nowadays...phew. Lemme tell you. We thought we were

47

cool in high school because we teased our hair high and wore dark eyeliner, or donned pink and green to catch the eye of our resident Jake Ryan. We thought winking was flirting, even when we looked like idiots after our heavily mascaraed eyelashes got stuck together. We wrote our crush notes and told all our friends so that, eventually, word would get back to him and *maybe* he would ask us out. How do they do it today? They just don't wear any clothes. Shorts are shorter, tops are practically non-existent and bralettes are the next big thing. That word, bralette, is even on my spell checker. If you don't know what I'm talking about, it's a bra where the kids wear the strap up behind their necks because they want it to be seen. Sure, in the 80's we wore lingerie as shirts but at least most of us covered it up with a cool jean jacket and wore at least one cool glove. How are we supposed to avoid lust? I don't know. I'm thinking about taking a cue from the Quakers and dressing her in a cotton dress that buttons at the neck and falls all the way to the floor, but then again, she will probably just sell it. I think this is just one of those things we have to accept will come and never go.

5. **Pride:** I struggle with this one, actually. We want our kids to be proud. We want them to take pride in their appearance, to wear appropriate clothes, to be proud when they get good grades or have some kind of accomplishment. We want them to be proud of their actions and be proud of their friends. But, what we don't want is for them to be jerks about it. We don't want them too overconfident, but we do

want them to have confidence. We want balance. So, for this one, I say go for it. The punishment in Hell is to be broken on the wheel. I'm not sure what that means exactly, but it sounds awful. I'm hoping for grace on this one, because, as far as I'm concerned, you go with your bad self.

6. **Envy:** This starts early on and gets worse and worse as time goes on. We're all envious. We're all jealous. But teenagers, well, they're taking home first place on this one. My daughter was a competitive gymnast. Not only is it one of the hardest sports to master, but you're on a team with the same people you're competing against. So, you're supporting and cheering on your teammates, but at the same time, you want to beat them. It's natural. And it doesn't just come from the kids, it comes from the parents. Parents tally up scores on their kid's

competitors during competition, some of them force them to practice at home after being in the gym five hours a day, some of them make them practice on broken bones, and some of them have panic attacks watching their kids compete. We want them to be winners. We want them to have a grasp on healthy competition. And then, we shove the pressure down their throats. I know, because I did it. I thought I was encouraging her, but really, I was feeding into her natural, animalistic, competitive nature and then wondering why she was acting like a shit when she didn't win. I have some good friends who are "Gym Moms" who have managed to instill the art of competition in their kids while teaching them how to be gracious, but some of these moms – wow. They'll even resort to buying their kids friends just to have a personal cheering section. We, as parents, are culpable here, folks. This is one of those "sins" we also need to work on. And, as I stand on my soap box, I am working on it too. I am trying to teach my kids that it's okay to lose and still come out on top. It's okay to get knocked down and get back up. It's okay to be jealous of somebody else, but it's not okay to be an asshole about it. Let it drive them to be better. Let it drive them to set goals and a plan to obtain them. Let defeat make them better. Let "want" make them work harder. If I can give you one piece of totally unsolicited advice on envy – be patient with this one. They'll get it, eventually. One day, as they come out of this freak of nature teenage thing and they blossom into beautiful young men and women, they will know how amazing they are. How talented. How beautiful—

in any form. They will know they are good enough, strong enough, and worthy of great things. Because, even when they're little heathens, you will tell them. In your own way, you will get that point across. Write it down if you have to. Tell them you love them. Write it in lipstick on their mirror if you can't utter the words because you're mad at them that day. Write it on the five-dollar bill they're gonna steal out of your wallet. Tell them they're valuable. Remind them that this shit is normal, and they will come out the other side. Because, I promise you, they will.

7. **Wrath:** They say "Hell hath no fury like a woman scorned." I don't know who "they" are, but "they" obviously don't have teenagers. Either that, or they have never seen a teenager pissed. And, do we ever really know

why? You know when they're mad at something. Slamming doors. Throwing down their backpacks. But they won't tell you what's wrong. No, it's the perpetual game of twenty questions that leaves you guessing until you're blue in the face. Then, somehow, it becomes your fault. You're to blame. Never mind that little Miss Popularity at school hurt their feelings or told the whole school their deepest, darkest secrets, or that the boy they liked asked another girl out. No. This is YOUR fault, and they will be the first ones to tell you that. Or show you that. I remember the first time I saw my youngest daughter really mad. It took everything I had not to laugh. And, I'm glad I didn't, because if I did, I think she was ready to kick my ass. Still, to this day, I don't really know what she was mad about it, but she sat in the recliner, with her legs crossed, kicking her crossed leg out into thin air, with fire in her eyes. And whatever it was that she was upset about didn't matter because I was at fault. For breathing, I think. Just being alive at that moment. Tears filled her eyes and her voice cracked, but there was no way she was going to tell me the real reason she was pissed. Nope. She was just mad. And then, my roommate walked in and she melted. What in the actual hell? She's mad at me because I exist, and he walks in and suddenly she's the sweet kid again. I think there is something about the mother/daughter, or even the mother/son, dynamic that just makes it happen. They might think they hate you, but really, they know how strong you are. They know you can shoulder their storm. They know you can take it. They know they can be shitty and you will love them

55

anyway. They know that you will always be there for them, even when you can't stand them in that moment. It's like childbirth. While you're in it, you promise yourself you will never have another baby again. No, fuck that. Ain't nothing coming out of that vagina ever again. And then you hold them and love them, and they smell so good, and nine months later, you're doing it again. Because you just don't give up, and kids sense that. I'm telling you, you're doing something right if they trust you enough to show you that vulnerable side to them. We just have to learn to appreciate that, even if we really want to run far, far away into the magical kingdom of, "I don't give a shit," where the skies are blue, money grows on trees, and margaritas are always within your grasp. Or for me, a martini. Tequila makes me sick.

Time for me to wrap up this chapter because my dog is barking and growling into thin air. I've told him to stop sixteen times, but he listens as well as my fifteen-year-old. In all seriousness, friends, try to remember back when you were a crazy kid. All those hormones, mixed messages, pressure, stress – it's all natural. They're going to get through it. And so are we.

What the hell has actually happened?
Never mind, let's get drunk.

I, literally, just got back from the mall after school shopping with my soon-to-be sophomore and her friend. It's only been a year since we tackled the stores for this event, but after today, I now know why Dads opt to go camping, roll around in elk urine, and shit in a hole rather than go to the mall three days before school starts. As if the crowds weren't bad enough, my girl decided to wear a flannel that hung lower than her shorts, pretty much making it look like she was walking around naked from the waist down. As soon as we walked into the first store, she was flocked by sales people who, I am sure, were calculating their commissions in their head. I mean, why not? Everybody wants to help the girl who comes in pant-less. Obviously, she needs some clothes.

Thank goodness it wasn't too painful. She grabbed a few things and off to the dressing room we went. There's a secret moms' club back there, you know. All the 40-something women who were probably well dressed in the 80's now sitting around in the big shirts and leggings, looking worn out and tired, repeating the same line, "Wait, you want me to buy you another white shirt after I spent $70.00 on the last one that you never wore?" When I heard that, I wanted to reach out and hug that mom. You know, offer her some comfort. I feel you, sister. Next time I go, I'm bringing mini bottles of alcohol to sell out of my purse to all the moms half smiling, half panicking about the bill they're about to receive. I can see it now. Me, sitting in the folding chair the chain store has provided, up against the wall, looking around at all the other moms holding a heap of clothes in their lap, kicking their crossed leg and scrolling Facebook trying to drown out the rap music in the background. At some point, one of them will look up, stretch their neck, and look my way where I will wink and point in my purse. She'll instinctively know. She will smile and pass me $20 as I wrap up a mini bottle of Jack Daniels in a T-shirt, pass it her way, and whisper "Hey, your daughter should try this shirt," *wink* *wink*. I quickly decided that I am going to open a store in the mall where moms can get pedicures and lounge on plush chairs while being served martinis by a shirtless Italian named "Lorenzo." I even invented little devices in my head where we can approve purchases from afar, never once having to leave to rummage through the sale racks. The service itself might be free with an upcharge for uber drivers on call and a breathalyzer that automatically halts your purchases when your blood alcohol level reaches a .08. I will not be responsible for some hungover mom the next day trying to read receipts while squinting, trying to get her Tylenol bottle open.

At one point, she mentioned to me, "You should get a pair of vans." Oh, sister, I had them. My generation invented them. Just because I walk around now in support shoes with odor inserts does not mean I wasn't cool at some point. Just because the guy at one of the kiosks passed over you and offered me some free wrinkle cream does not mean I was not cool. It took everything I had not to shout it out, "I was cool once! I was cool once! Dammit!" Okay, even if I wasn't, your dad was. He was cool. He was *so* cool.

I remember being a teenager going to the mall with my mom. You know, walking two steps ahead or three steps behind. I was lucky my mom was a reader and could sit for hours in the dressing rooms reading her books, and I was thankful she didn't actually vomit every time she thought she might when she saw the bill. And while I was sitting in one of the stores today with my own child, Big Brother must have been watching because, as I was reminiscing about my teenager-hood, "You Might Think" by the Cars came on the speakers overhead just in time for me to hear my sweet girl shriek in delight proclaiming, "These are so cool!" What, you might ask, was she referring to? I had to look twice as I saw her holding, none other than, a fanny pack. Yes, a fucking fanny pack! And they're cool now! What? Some days she can pretty much hate every move I make but, suddenly, the shit from our youth, like Vans and fanny packs, are cool? Not just that, but guess what else is back? Rainbow shirts. Yes, all my 40ish year old friends. Rainbow shirts. I need not say more. Life is complete.

And, guess what else? They think they invented joggers. Ha, ha. Ask MC Hammer about parachute pants.

But one thing I didn't do as a kid was shop at Victoria's Secret. Maybe there wasn't one around. Maybe it was just for adults. All I can remember is, if you wanted anything but a six pack of bikini cut undies from Sears, you had to somehow convince your mom to drive you to "Frederick's of Hollywood," which wasn't happening in my house. Well, now they have "Pink" and it's the place to go. I couldn't help but chuckle at the fact that, there we were in a lingerie shop and she's searching for thongs while I am looking for perfume. When did I become an adult? What has happened here? When did the "days of the week" panties go out of style? SHE STOLE MY LIFE.

I'm not that old! I mean it was just yesterday I was at the mall with my friends, people watching and being dumb and shopping for the latest, cutest pair of overalls. Now, the teenage sales people are talking about what version of the keto diet they're on and how they need to lose weight. What the fuck happened to "Hot Dog on a Stick" and since when do you need to lose weight when you're already a size 3? Now, you have to make sure you get the jeans with all the holes in them. Like, you actually pay for jeans with holes in them. Not little holes. No. Big ones. And not just in the knee. All the way up their fucking thighs! And not a hole they earned from playing hard or working hard either. Just holes. Rips. All over. Now, we're paying a hundred dollars for them not to be pre-shrunk, but to be pre-ripped! Remember when we were kids and we patched the fucking holes? I actually remember going to the fabric store (remember when our moms made us clothes?) and begging my mom to buy me patches so I didn't have to throw my jeans away. Because once they had holes in them, they became UNUSABLE, unless we cut them and made jean shorts out of them. But, even then you had to cut them above the rip and sometimes they were too short to wear in public. Three inches above the knee was pushing it, but now, these kids are wearing shorts that don't cover any more than a bikini bottom does. And not only that, but then their pockets are hanging out under the jeans and onto their thigh. How the fuck are they supposed to carry their keys or illegal cigarettes or pot in there? I try not to judge the girls who wear shorts with their asses hanging out. I am sure they are nice kids, but man, I'm pretty sure Mr. Levi Strauss is turning over in his grave.

I did have to laugh though when I thought she got stuck in the dressing room for a minute. I flashed back to the time she accidentally locked herself in the pantry. Oh, how I should have slipped her math homework in there and told her she could come out when it was done.

Remember when we went to the mall and had to have an actual note from our parents to use their credit card? Not anymore. Oh no, these kids can just waltz right in and tap their iPhone for their purchase and nobody really cares. Remember when we used to go to the mall and we went to actually go shopping? The girls dress up now like they're going a club, people. I'm surprised they don't charge a cover and give them wristbands and have bouncers in the food court. Speaking of food courts, I am serious when I ask what happened to Hot Dog on a Stick. Seeing your friends wearing those striped uniforms and silly hats jumping up and down on lemons to make lemonade was the highlight of my day. Now, it's organic this and organic that. But, then again, I guess these kids need to eat organic if they're going to be wearing a string for underwear and bralettes instead of a real bra. You know, the kind that actually keep your boobs in place. I guess they will figure it out when they're 40 trying to tape up two pounds of fat in their chest wishing they had invested in some underwire. And it's not just the girls. Let's be clear on that. I saw a boy in capri pants. Is that a thing? Is he going fishing? Wading through some water maybe? I don't mean long board shorts. I mean actual capri pants, like I wear. And please, boys, cut your hair. A "man-bun" is not a style. I swear. It's not. Unless you're a Samurai, there's just no need for it because when the captain of the football team goes to kick your ass for wearing girl pants, it's the first thing he's gonna grab. Be smart. Protect yourself.

I just don't remember us being like this, I honestly don't. But, then again, I guess our parents had the same complaints about our clothes, our music, and our habits. I feel like I need to write my mom an apology letter for all the hell I put her through. Maybe I can attach one of the pictures we did at Glamor Shots. Do they do that anymore? Do you remember? It was quite the treat to get your make-up and hair done at the mall, but the problem was not only did everybody have the same outfits on, but we all had the same hair. Curly for short hair girls, wavy for long hair girls. It's probably not around anymore because who needs it when you have Instagram and Snap-Chat filters.

Don't tell anybody, but I secretly love the filters. They're fun. Silly. You can be a dog if you want to, wear a mustache, be an alien, sometimes a bunny, and you can have really cool battle of the filters contests with your teenager. I don't care how mad at me she is, or how much she thinks I don't understand—challenge her to a Snap-Chat filter contest and we're BFFs again.

Oh yes, teenagers. I never thought I would be *that* mom. You know, the one who walked around half confused by them. No, I was going to be the cool mom, the one who "got it," the one who my kids could identify with, the one who my kids were always honest with, who they never fought with, who they saw as somebody who really understood them. But, I guess this whole mom/dad/teenager/what the fuck are you doing thing is a rite of passage and one we are just going to have to laugh our way through. We might not laugh as hard as we did looking back at pictures of us in bicycle shorts and T-shirts, or when we remember the long summer days when we tanned in the middle of the backyard using baby oil on our skin and lying on tin foil, or teasing our hair up as high as it would go, or layering our socks different colors, or wishing our crush would invite us to the next "John Hughes" movie, only to be too scared to go with them alone so we had to convince them to set up their friend with our friend before we would say yes.

I hate to break it to you moms and dads, but we were just as dumb, but at least MTV actually played music. We wore stupid shit. We did stupid things. We talked like valley girls and broke the rules. We had some pretty awful music and maybe we didn't text, but we spent just as much time passing notes. Yes, my friends. I hate to break this to you, but we were assholes, too.

I can't wait until she's my age. I'm going to give her kids money to shop at the mall and tell them their mom would LOVE to take them. And when mom calls me 15 hours later crying, I'm going to sit back, put my feet up, sip my martini, and laugh my ass off. Yep, sure am. I can't wait to be a Grandma asshole.

"Stop Touching Me"

Sometimes, I seriously wonder if it's only my kids that fight. Or, maybe it was just me and my brother. I mean, in today's day and age and if you believe social media, all kids (even teenagers) are tiny angels who sleep, eat, play on cue, and not only have matching outfits but never make a mess.

Annnnnd then….I remember Cain and Abel. I imagine Eve spent a lot of time chasing after them screaming things like, "Put down that rock!", "Who gave you that spear?", "No need for that kind of jealousy!", "Yes, you ARE your brother's keeper and not only will you do it, but you *will* like it!" Back then, not only could Eve have really carried out the act that went along with, "I brought you into this world and I can take you out!", but I'm pretty sure it would have been legal for her to go through with the whole "eye for an eye" thing too.

Not like now where if your kid is mad at you and you happen to brush shoulders with them in the hallway, they think the police are going to swoop in and arrest you for child abuse. Let me be clear, folks. That ideology is not because your kid is an asshole. It's the adult somewhere who told them that who is an asshole. It's the legislator who doesn't want to let you parent your kid who is an asshole. Anyway, moving on…

Yes, sibling rivalry. It's a tale as old as time and with the exception of the Cain and Abel type stories, it can be pretty funny.

There comes a point where those phrases, "He's touching me," "She's looking at me," "He's copying me," "She's breathing on me," go from, "Please stop fighting," to "Oh, shut the fuck up," to hysterical laughter. Maybe delusional laughter. Nervous, need-to-be-committed laughter. I guess we get to a point where we really don't give a fuck anymore about who's right and who's wrong. All we want is quiet.

I published an article today about kids, mostly about teenagers. Some lady left a comment about how she was raising her kids one way and how she wasn't going to do this or do that. I couldn't help but look over her Facebook and, exactly what I expected: she's the mother of toddlers. I laughed. Oh man, I laughed. I love it when toddler moms have some kind of prediction on how their kids are going to turn out because of what that mom is "gonna do." Ummmmm, okay toddler mom superstar. I was "gonna" too. I had sweet toddlers too. They sat at the kitchen table and did homework. They had fruit and cheese for snacks. They wore cute pajamas. They wanted to help around the house. They took naps. They snuggled. They had tiffs with their siblings which were quickly worked through with a talking lesson and a hug.

And then, somewhere along the line, they became assholes and not only did they want to beat on each other, but I wanted to beat on them. That toddler mom told me that my kid must "rule the roost" and oh, my, yes, the laughing. YES, THE KIDS RULE THE ROOST AND YOURS DO TOO.

You can say they don't, but they do. I guarantee it. Every time you aren't drinking a glass of wine from your personal wine cellar, sitting on your veranda overlooking your 100 acres of pure peace and quiet but, instead, reading "Horton Hears a Who" for the 500th time, it's because YOUR kid is ruling your roost.

Your kids are going to demand, they're going to be jerks, they're going to grow up, they're going to push your buttons, and they're going to fight. The best thing you can do is find the humor in it. This is the best piece of advice I can give you other than if you can't laugh, you might as well just check yourself into a mental institution now.

Yes, siblings. Ah, siblings. The good, the bad, and the ugly. Way ugly sometimes. I often wonder why we have multiple kids. I think it's because the first one is so new and sweet and, most of the time, they're easy. Not all of the time, but really, when you think about it, all your focus is on them. You don't have to worry about a gaggle of crying, spaghetti throwing thugs and you can just love on them. Everything is fun. First coos, first laughs, first words, first steps. I look back now and realize what a trap that was—we spend all this time trying to teach them how to walk and talk and then, four years later, all we want them to do is shut up and sit down for five minutes straight. I used to tell my kids to pretend they were a tree. Just stand there. Be a tree. Trees don't move. Trees don't talk. It didn't take long for them to realize I was full of shit and then, suddenly, the tree was touching "hot lava" and, well, you know how that goes.

Anyway, first babies are awesome. My first was textbook easy. She nursed well, she met all her milestones before she was supposed to, or right on time. She was so sweet. So cute. She let me dress her up. It's a miracle she learned to walk because I carried her everywhere. I just wanted to be with her all the time. My mom joked that when I asked her to watch the baby, that's exactly what she did—just watched the baby. It was heavenly. Nothing could change my mind about how wondrous babies were. Until the second one came along, and then the third. I swear, I don't know one mom who doesn't have a prescription for some kind of tranquilizer once they have three kids. There's something magical about that number, I think. One, two, three strikes and you're definitely out. And then there are people who think, "Oh, let's just even it out and have four." Are you crazy? You know you're building their team right? I mean, in a two-parent household, there are only two of you, which means you're outnumbering yourself—ON PURPOSE. Forfeit. Now. Take one off the field.

Because when they get older, and all the grandeur fades away, they fight. *ABOUT EVERYTHING.*

Now that my kids are almost all grown-ups, I can look back at my life with them and laugh at some things. But, not at the time. No, they are lucky to be alive. Quite literally in some cases because, when your son falls through the ceiling because he wanted to "explore" the attic, your first thought is not, "Oh, honey are you okay?", it's "Why in the hell are you in the attic and let me see the damage." I remember that call so vividly. I was at work and got a phone call from my son's friend who could not, for the life of him, spit out what happened. He said something like, "Um, um…" *Just say it, kid, I'm busy.* "Yeah, so, um, well, he went through the ceiling."

"What?!?"

Click. The little shit hung up. I'm assuming he was terrified and put up to delivering the news by my own kid, but it freaked me out. I called my older daughter who, very matter of fact, told me that he and his friends wanted to explore the attic and he fell through it. He was fine, but there was a gaping hole in the ceiling. This was one of the only times I was glad she tattled on him, because, in this case, I needed the head's up. My son would not get on the phone with me, but he did call my late husband and ask if he should move out. I don't know how their conversation went, but I do know that while my son was up there, he found a tool my husband was missing so, apparently, it was A-Okay. I got home that night and there it was, in all its glory.

A huge hole in the ceiling, with insulation all over the floor. My son and his friends sat there with stupid grins on their faces, but, shaking because they were terrified. All I could tell them was to "clean it up," which they did, yet I still don't think they understand that using masking tape to hold up the drywall wasn't going to work for very long. I think it's safe to assume that my older daughter probably told them not to go up there, but in true sibling fashion – he didn't listen.

Those two were something. That's for sure. I think deep down they loved each other, but she didn't love it when he terrorized her. It all started when my youngest was born, and when she was about eighteen months old, he decided it would be a great idea to recycle her poop, wad it up into a ball, and throw it at his older sister's door. I heard the screaming. I heard the door slamming. But never in my wildest dreams did I think I would walk upstairs and see a game of poop dodgeball. My little one thought it was fantastic. She was giggling and having a grand old time. Until they had to clean it up. I mean, my brother and I fought too, but not like that. I don't ever remember throwing poop around. I remember being told I hit him on the back of the head with the claw of a hammer when I was two. Come on, I was two. But, my poor mother. If she only knew it was a sign of things to come.

Oh, we fought, like two wet cats. I don't even know why. I'll tell you he was mean to me. He will tell you I was mean to him. I'm surprised my mom isn't an alcoholic. Besides the hammer story, I think it all started when my brothers were young and pretending they were football players. Somehow, they coaxed me into crawling into a tall laundry basket, you know the 70's wicker ones, and closing the lid while they tackled it. I don't know what those things are called in football, but you know the thing the coach stands on, and the players like run as fast as they can and slam their shoulders into it and try to move it? Yeah, that. They were pretending the laundry basket was that thing, and I guess they needed the weight inside. So much fun. Not. But for some stupid reason, I kept getting in. I guess that's the rule of siblings, we just keep doing stupid stuff together.

At one point, I started dreading answering the phone at work when my kids were in middle school. I think it came after my daughter called me and said that her brother wouldn't stop throwing snowballs at her. I told her, very reasonably, that if she didn't want to be hit with snowballs, that maybe she should go inside. She responded with, "I am inside." Well, shit. So was he. With the snow.

I honestly think he did things just to piss her off. Like it was some kind of rite of passage. When she started driving, the rule was she had to take him to school. Free gas, free insurance, she just had to take her kid brother with her. So, what did he do?

He took two-hour showers, likely, just to make her late. He knew this would frustrate her because she was an academic and all she wanted to do was go to school. I asked my husband why he would take two-hour showers just to piss her off and he disagreed that he was taking long showers to piss her off, but had something else going on in there, and gross—change the subject.

I know my older daughter had it rough with her wild brother. She was the "good kid." I mean hell, she even grounded herself one time. Not kidding, she handed over her car keys and her cell phone to my husband and told him to give them back to her when he thought she learned her lesson. Not thinking the issue at hand was a big deal, and it wasn't, he left them on the counter and told her to come back and get then when *she* thought she learned her lesson. I swear, I think they stayed there for three days.

My kids are adults now and not too long ago my older daughter traveled back east to where my son is stationed. They posted a picture of themselves together witch hunting in Salem, Massachusetts. While I was horrified by the fact that I raised two little traitors who would go witch hunting without me, I was beaming with joy knowing that all the drama, finger pointing, tattle telling, crying, meltdowns, and torture were over. It took a really long time. Lots of tears. Lots of talking. Lots of door slamming. Lots of glares and sticking out tongues. But in the end, they went witch hunting. That's a win in my book.

And besides, they've given me all these stories to tell their kids. That, in and of itself, made it all worth it.

Dads, Grammas, Aunts, Friends and Shit

The older my kids got, the more I noticed Dad walking around like a deer in the headlights with a permanent look of panic and fear settled into his eyes when he would get home from work.

Like the mighty warrior who is alert to every sound in the forest, he darts his eyes left to right, always vigilant to the location of the beast that might try to pounce on him. I see as he pauses before each corner in the hallway, carefully assessing the potential attack that could be before him as he stealthily makes his way into the house. Careful not to disturb the native, he quietly drops his used Tupperware from work into the sink and then slips out into the bedroom, relatively unnoticed. On the occasions where she sees him, where she catches him mid-Tupperware-drop, Dad knows there are only two options. Their eyes lock. Their hearts pound into their necks. Their blood turns to fire. Their muscles tense. He knows he has to be still and to let her make the first move.

Will it be an attack? Is he taking his last breaths? Will she break eye contact and walk slowly by, half smiling with evil dripping from her lips? Will she squint, smile, and wink like she has consumed her prey? Will she begrudgingly let down her guard for the sake of her wet laundry that she has to walk down the hall to switch to the dryer? Will she… will she…

Oh, who the fuck am I kidding? That's my scenario.

Rewind to where Dad is dropping his Tupperware. She steps down the stairs, peeks around the wall to make sure the sound she hears is him. They do lock eyes, but she does not growl. The smoke from her ears retracts. The shadow that surrounds her is sucked away. She is suddenly dressed in a white cotton sleeveless gown with lace around the neck, barefoot with the exception of the fairies that circle her feet. She adorns a crown of wildflowers with small birds that once belonged to Snow White, happily frolicking and singing around her precious, flowing locks of golden spun hair. She smiles. A childish, loving smile as she skips in to the kitchen to embrace him. He swings her around in delight after the eight-hour absence.

Alright, maybe there aren't really forest animals, but you get the picture.

She likes him better.

My daughter lost her dad a couple of years ago and it was traumatic for everybody. There is a love that daughters have for their dads that is inexplicably pure. It's untainted. The teenage daughter can pretty much hate everything in the whole world, but when it comes to their dad, they're madly in love. After he died, I met somebody. I'm not going to lie, it was weird. We were all adjusting to this new life and figuring out where we all fit and what our roles were. My youngest daughter was cautious in the beginning but, eventually, something clicked and before I knew it, they were best friends. At first, I was a little jealous of their relationship. When we first started dating, they would have FROYO dates. For those of you not in the know, that's frozen yogurt. They toured our city for the best FROYO places around and even had a little rating system to judge what was great and what wasn't. I was invited to tag along a handful of times, but I quickly realized there was something special going on there. Something between them, and it didn't include me. I witnessed the bonding and, while I wanted to be part of that in some way, I knew deep down I needed to let them have those moments alone.

He has been steadfast in his love for her since. Sure, he can get angry with her teenage antics, but it never causes him to not hug her when he sees her. He might be scared sometimes of the fifteen-year-old craziness, but he never hides.

As with any teenage girl, there are ups, downs, and a hormonal roller coaster that flips everything on its head. Sometimes I want to fall out of the roller coaster. That's when I am comforted by the fact that he sees her brokenness and loves her anyway. He brought her peace, comfort, and happiness when she needed it the most. And for that, she trusts him with her heart. No matter what life throws at them.

Don't get me wrong. I love my kids. I would do anything for them. Absolutely anything. But a mother/daughter relationship can be complicated. Maybe some of you don't have that issue so you can just turn the page, but for those of us who do, it's okay to take a step back and let somebody else love them. In fact, it's often necessary.

Because in those moments when you look at them and see all of yourself in them, all of your attitude and personality and are overwhelmed by your worries and fears, you want to have a back-up. You want to have somebody who can love them when you don't even really like them at that moment.

For me, sometimes, it's my friends. Sometimes, it's her friends. Sometimes, it's her siblings. For you, it might be their bio dad or a friend or another relative. Let them have it. Let them embrace it. Let them succeed where you might fail.

It's okay.

It's important.

It's a gift in the middle of the "what the fuck is happening" phase.

It doesn't mean your kid doesn't love you. It doesn't mean they don't care about you. It doesn't mean they don't want you. It doesn't mean they don't need you. Oh, they need you, that's for sure. They're going to need $20.00 before you know it, and you're going to be there. Timmy is going to break their heart and you're going to be the one who understands. They're going to need a dress for prom and it's you who is going to take them shopping. And they're going to love you that day. Not because you spent money on them but because, for that moment, you were their person.

Because while mother/daughter relationships are complicated, they're also magical.

For FROYO dates? That might be somebody else.

It's taken some time for me to realize that, and it's also taken me some time to realize that maybe your back-up isn't going to understand everything. Maybe they are going to be confused by your decisions. Maybe they are not going to understand the game of ping pong you guys play; one minute you're snuggling on the couch and the next you're ready to drop her off at the nearest fire station. Maybe they're just never going to understand any of it.

But it doesn't matter as long as they love her in such a way that she knows she always has somebody in her corner and somebody who will take her for frozen yogurt when life gets tough.

I'm sure my boyfriend often asked himself, "what the fuck did I get myself into," but I also know that he can laugh with the best of them, get the joke, understand that it's temporary and what a huge role he has in the shaping of this beautiful young woman.

I hope your person, no matter who that is, does that for the kid you love.

I hope they don't get too scared, never run away, and always have garlic and a cross on hand just in case.

I also hope that you and your person have a good, but selective memory. I hope you can forget most of the shit you've been tossed but remember the funny stories. Because there's nothing like a grandma and grandpa sitting by a fire, holding their grandkids in their laps telling them about the time their mom almost gave him a heart attack.

Aw yes, good times. Good times.

My Kid Is an Asshole, and So Is My Dog

Let's talk about those dogs.

I try to avoid talking about the dogs very often. I mean, I like them and all, but they pretty much drive me nuts. If they weren't so damn cute, it might be different. They're Shih Tzu's and if you have ever seen one, you know they never really grow out of the puppy-looking phase. The problem is, I don't think their brains ever grow up either. Currently, one of them is sleeping in his doggie bed with his body in the bed and his head hanging off the side onto the floor. The other one, well, he's just looking around trying to figure out if he's alive. I would like to say they do something cool, like maybe they're "tracking dogs," but the fact is, the only thing they track is my burrito.

The one who I am not sure knows he's alive? He's now "cleaning" his stuffed animal. Like, licking it. As if it were his puppy. It's not even a stuffed puppy. It's a stuffed owl. But even if it were a real puppy, how would he not know that it's probably dead? It never moves. Never cries. Oh, that's right, because Karl doesn't know he's alive either.

Yes, his name is Karl, with a K. I actually used to talk about him a lot. So much so, people thought my husband's name was Karl. I would go to work and people would ask me, "So, what did you and Karl do this weekend?" I thought it was weird but didn't want to be rude. "Oh, you know, same ol', same ol'. I got things done around the house while he just walked around my feet and licked his balls." Strange how nobody ever said anything in response to that. Maybe they just didn't know how to respond to a woman telling them that their husband sat on the couch and cleaned himself while I made a pot roast.

I didn't name him, by the way. That was my husband, Chad, with a C. He's named after the character "Karl" in "Slingblade," and Karl has totally lived up to his name. If he could talk, I am sure the only things he would say would absolutely be, "mmmhmm," and "I like them French fried

93

potaters." The other dog, well, that there is Cleatus. Or, is it Cletus? I don't even know how to spell it. I have no idea why that's his name but before we had him and had real, human kids, he told me that if I had a boy, he was going to name him Cletus. *Oh no, he wasn't.* He even threatened to beat me to the birth certificate lady, to which I vowed that even with a C-section, he would not win. I would flop my numb body out of the hospital bed and army crawl down the hallway if I had to.

I want it noted that I didn't buy either dog. When my kid was struggling with sleeping through the night as a toddler, he thought it would be a great idea to bribe her and tell her if she slept in her bed for 90 days straight, he would buy her a puppy. 90 days came and went and off they ventured to find the perfect pup. He was a cop. I figured he was coming home with a German shepherd or a Doberman Pincher, yet after three hours or so, he saunters in with a Shih Tzu. A little black and white Shih Tzu. It was all fun and games until, two years later, he showed up with Cletus. A blonde Shih Tzu who, on day two, fell off the landing of the stairs and hit his head. He's never been right since. He thinks he's a bulldog. He has this huge underbite, his arms are kinda bow-shaped, and he bulldozes his way through everything. One thing he is really good at though, is barking. Every night at 4:00 and 11:00, without fail. I have no idea what he's barking at, but he runs outside and barks. On the nights when I can't catch him quick enough, yeah, I'm sure my neighbors love me. It's not as bad when he's howling like Chewbacca, but still. He's not a Wookie. I don't know how to get that through his very thick skull. I guess Karl is my favorite because, when he finally has an alert moment and he knows he's actually here on earth, he's super cute and friendly and cuddly. Cletus just kinda stares at you, trying to figure out if he should bark at you. One thing Cletus can do though that Karl can't, is catch food. I don't mean like wild game or anything, but he can catch food you throw at him. No matter what it is, he will catch it.

French fries, pieces of meat, chicken, small children, you know. Everything.

After we got Cletus, I was perfectly happy with just the two. We were a sweet nuclear family, but just like all idiotic parents, we figured that since everything had gone so well with the first two dogs, why not get a third? It's kinda like having a third kid. You think it sounds really great at the time. After all, you got this down pat. The kids (or the dogs) listen. They've figured out the routine. They're pretty predictable. Every now and then they screw up, but everybody learns from it. They're kinda messy, but not too bad. You can still take them out in public. Your friends are used to them.

Then, enter the third. In my case, the third dog and the third kid were not all that different.

They came in, looked around, and settled in. Oh, they were so cute. They smelled good. They cuddled. They needed me. I protected them from the other two. We got to know each other. I wanted them to feel safe. Comfortable. Welcomed.

Then, without warning, they took over. Both of them. Like Tasmanian devils, as soon as they could walk on their own, it was over. Furniture chewed on. Toilet paper strewn around the house. Food spilled. Foreign liquids stamped in the carpet. Demands for food, water, shelter, sometimes clothes. Upsetting the balance. The flow. The way it worked. And just when you were ready to return them, they extend an olive branch. The kid brings you a weed they picked in the backyard thinking it was a flower and mumble the words, "I wuv you," while the dog brings you a lizard tail and licks your face before you realize he dropped it behind the couch. Either way, your heart melts. So, you let them stay and twelve hours later, the cycle repeats.

My third dog, Claire, was also a Shih Tzu. Another bribe by the husband to the kid. It was more of a joke than anything, but one that backfired on him. Totally backfired. So much so, I giggled for hours. He was going to have three dogs. Not me. Oh no, him. Yeah, I laughed. A lot. At least until he died and then I was stuck with the fucking thing. My daughter was competing in an international gymnastics meet one year in Las Vegas. There was little chance she would win for her age and skill level. After all, she was a kid from Idaho just bouncing off the walls. So, he thought it would be a great idea to "motivate" (ahem, bribe) her by telling her that if she won, he would buy her ANOTHER dog. He didn't think she would win, but what he forgot was that she is her father's daughter and when met with a challenge, she's probably going to do it. And she did. She won.

I remember watching the color drain from his face. I remember this because I was in hysterics. Sucker. Except he ended up having the last laugh. He died and left me with the damn thing. All three of them. And the kid. Yeah, real funny, babe. Real funny.

Claire didn't last long. She escaped. Straight to Gramma's house.

My Kid Is an Asshole, and So Is My Dog

So, now, she has a cat. Not kidding. I don't have a cat but, apparently, she does. She can't scrape together $2.00 in quarters but, somehow, she can find $10.00 to buy a cat. Seriously? I guess she doesn't know that she can just go outside and find one? For FREE? I don't go into her room very often. Mostly from fear of contracting some kind of airborne disease from old pizza boxes and dirty socks. But, the other day, I had to take my life in my own hands and wake her up. It was easy enough, but then I forgot something and had to go back in. Imagine my surprise as I witnessed her hopping back into bed with a kitten in her hands. It was surreal. In slow motion. I had to blink over and over to make sure I was seeing it correctly. I think I heard "Chariots of Fire" playing in the background. As she flopped back on the bed, I saw it. A little gray face with this tiny "meow" coming from its mouth. I actually gasped. She smiled as the little shit purred and tucked its perfect little kitty head under her chin.

I did a quick assessment of the room. Food bowl, check. Water bowl, check. I immediately wondered who is supplying food for this feline. Turns out her friends are smuggling in cat food like the Columbian Cartel. Then it dawned on me that a few days prior, one of her friends brought over a fish to give to her and, suddenly, I couldn't help the horrific thoughts pouring through my head that there's some kind of animal fight club happening in her room. I suppose I should have checked on the fish but, at the time, I was guessing it was here on some kind of visitation or something since I never saw a fish bowl. Yeah…it was in her bathroom. Of course, it was. I don't know why I'm shocked, after all, she had a fucking four-legged mammal in her room for two weeks. For all I know, there's a llama in her closet.

I assumed nobody knew about the cat, but it seems the roommate had an idea when she asked him for one of the dog kennels "for a friend." He thought it was suspicious, but I guess never thought he should ask if she needed it to sneak in a kitten. Boy, does he have a lot to learn. Sometimes I feel sorry for him but, mostly, I just wonder if he has any common sense.

For a millisecond I thought maybe I would let her keep the cat. After all, she's had a lot of loss already. But, not only am I allergic, I have two dogs already who are assholes that she loves and "can't live without" until it comes time to pick up their poop or buy food or anything else. I don't want a cat. I dunno, maybe some moms would have "oohed" and "awed" and loved the damn thing. Maybe I am just a bad mom. Maybe I am heartless. She comes by this naturally, you know. Her dad snuck in animals, too, when he was a kid. But his mom was nice enough to let him keep them.

I texted my older kids to see if they ever set up a zoo in their rooms. So far, no answer. Chickens. I sincerely hope none of them had snakes. Or rats. OMG, I can't even think about it.

I'm pretty sure I never brought an animal home. A few boyfriends maybe, but never an actual creature. I don't know why other than I didn't want to take care of one, and I still don't. I mean, I kinda like the dogs from time to time but when they go, they're not being replaced. I don't have empty nest syndrome and I am not going to acquire it anytime soon. When the last kid is out, I have big plans. You know, sleep in, cook and not do dishes, know where all my stuff is, change the locks, be spontaneous, go on vacation--you know, live the life. But if she keeps bringing animals here, I have a feeling they're going to always live here, even when she's gone. I am just happy my backyard isn't big enough for a horse. Hey, mini-me, if you're reading this, IT IS NOT BIG ENOUGH FOR A HORSE.

I got rid of the cat. I gave it to a friend and $200 later after shots, food, and fixing the fucker, I am free of that responsibility.

Until the other day, when my roommate said something about the cat. I figured he meant the old cat or was kidding. He wasn't. I stood at the bottom of the stairs and could not believe I was hearing another little "meow" sound coming from her room.

ANOTHER kitten.

Shoot me. Just shoot me.

Apparently, she REALLY wants a cat. I marched right up there ready to kick them both out, flung open the door, and there it was looking me square in the eye.

A perfect little black and white kitten with a mustache. Like, a real, little mustache. Well, it kinda looks like a sideways exclamation point, but it's a mustache nonetheless. We stared at each other, sizing each other up. My heart melted a little bit. It was cute, I thought. Like, dangerously cute. It looked a lot like Karl. Except as a cat. A cat Karl. I just hope this one knows she's alive.

Because I let her keep it. I know, more bad Parenting 101 by me, but ignorance is not bliss, folks. Ignorance is toxoplasmosis and scratched up bedding. And, dare I say it: newborn kittens. I realized she's just going to keep bringing cats home until I let her have one. I know how many people are shaking their heads right now, but I'm trying to pick and choose my battles here. And besides, I make her take it with her wherever she goes. Going to a friend's? Take the cat. Going on a date? Take the cat. Going for ice cream? Take the cat.

Maybe dragging the cat around everywhere she goes will get so inconvenient, she won't want to drag a toddler around anytime soon.

I actually wish we had the fucking cat in our old house when we had a mouse problem. We spent more time killing mice than we did anything else. That was, until we found a newborn mouse outside on the sidewalk and nursed it to health. My daughter couldn't stand the fact of just letting it sit there and die, so we actually protected and fed the damn thing until it was old enough to live on its own and run into a mouse trap.

On a side note, I don't understand why my dogs ever try to run away when the front door opens.

I assume they want to feel the air flow through their hair but, the next time they bolt out of the door, I am not going after them. I have run after them far too many times in a towel and wet hair for my liking. I don't know what they're running from anyway. They've got it made with me. Full tummies, lots of cuddling, hair styles, sweaters in the winter, owl toys. I have no idea what's wrong with all of that. Maybe they have PTSD from the time my husband accidentally overdosed them, but still, it wasn't that bad. Just because he mixed up their medication after they got their tally whacker's cut off and walked around bumping into walls for three days, does not mean they're not happy. After five years, Karl's face finally looks somewhat normal now and Cletus' drooling has stopped, so they're fine. I think my husband was more horrified from the fact that he sent out a group text that was only supposed to come to me saying, *"I think I killed the dogs,"* than he was that the dogs had to eat charcoal to throw up. If keeping the dogs awake wasn't bad enough, he had to spend all afternoon responding to the condolence texts that shortly followed.

But remember the cat? They're trying to kill it. I am so scared I am going to come home one day to find one of their eyes sitting on the floor. I decided to be pro-active and put up a baby gate at the top of the stairs, but the only one I had handy had metal slats in it. I figured the cat could get through it, but surely wasn't stupid enough to try with the beasts on the other side. No. She wasn't. But the dogs were dumb enough to try to get to her. Yep. Only Karl's head fit through, and of course, it wouldn't come out.

I was at work.

The kid tried to lather him up with Crisco. A Shih Tzu. Bathed in lard.

I told her to call me when the dog was out. I waited patiently.

Thirty minutes later, she sent me a picture of the fire department cutting the damn dog out of the gate.

106

I have no idea why anybody wonders why my motto is, "fuck me," and why I think they're all assholes.

The shit my kid says

Dear Parents,

It's not just my kid. Oh no, it's your kid too. I thought you might need this handy reference guide to understand your teenager and the shit they're saying, so I asked my teenager and her friend, Bridgette, for some examples. The following is Bridgette's list. Apparently, my kid was too busy being low key and had to dip.

1.   Lit:

So, basically, this means "cool." I *think* before they would say "legit" instead of "lit." I'm not sure what happened. Maybe they got tired of having to sound out two whole syllables.

2.   Shoot Brotha:

"Crap," "Dang It," "Shoot." That's what it means. And, apparently, they're all gangsters.

3.   Okur:

They say this means "Okay." I get that but the way they say it around these parts, it sounds like an elk call, not a confirmation. I don't think I can even describe it in words but I'm gonna try. First of all, it should be spelled, "Oooookkkkkuuurttttttttt." And, the octave in their screechy voices goes up at the end. And they roll the "R." It's extremely annoying and a lot of work on their part. But now I know why they had to shorten "legit." They obviously had to save their energy to get this thing out.

4. Bruh

"Dude." I think they think they made this up.

5. AF:

How old were you when you figured out AF was NOT short for "Abercrombie & Fitch?" Me? I was today years old. It means "As fuck." Yep, they drop the f-bomb too. Shocker.

6. Thirsty:

Desire for something sexual. Look, I am just trying to help so don't get mad at me. I'm just saying, that if Billy and the boys are hanging out in your kitchen eating Subway sandwiches and their drinks are full, but they're still saying they're "thirsty," they might not be talking about Dr. Pepper.

7.   Throwing shade:

"Dissing" someone or something. I don't get it. Shade is a bad thing? Please throw me some! I want to find some shade and take a fucking nap.

8.   Savage:

Doing something you probably shouldn't but still doing it because you don't care what anyone thinks. I'm not sure if they described "savage" or ex-boyfriend.

9.   Squad:

111

Your group of friends. This one makes total sense.

10. Salty:

When somebody is being bitter. It's funny. I think my late husband made this up. He was the only person I have ever heard use this term for YEARS. People didn't know what it meant, and we always explained it like the look on your face when you eat something really salty. So glad this generation gets it!

11. Shook:

Shocked about something. Let's just say I named her illegal cat "Shook."

12. Looking like a snack:

I'm not even going to define it. I am just going to leave this right here. But, I will tell you—they're not hungry for food.

13. High Key:

"I don't care who knows." Code for: Put it on social media. And, tag me.

14. Low Key:

"Keep it confidential." Code for: Put in on social media. Don't tag me but start that rumor anyway.

15. Dip:

"To leave." No lie, I am going to start using this one.

16. Finna:

"To go do something." Wait. That's not even a word. Do you mean "fixin'?"

17. Geekin:

"The action of laughing." In my day, if you laughed too hard, you were "gleeking."

18. Basic:

"Someone or something is ordinary or boring." They're talking about parents.

19. Clouds:

"The vapor from your vape." I can't tell you how happy I am that somebody, somewhere told these kids vaping was cool.

114

20. Bud:

"Weed." Again, one I think they think they made up. We all know, kids. Look, Bruh, most of us were raised in the 80's. We all know you're not talking about meeting your friend, "Bud" at the Dairy Queen. Just like we weren't meeting ours under the bleachers during P.E.

You're welcome.

115

Why We Don't Go on Vacation?

I'm not even going to write a chapter on this. I am just going to include the e-mail I sent my mom the last time my husband and I tried to take all the kids camping and let you use your imagination. I wish I would have apologized better for being the same assholic teen.

Dear Mom,

I just wanted to thank you for the camping memories. I wish I could transport Stephen, Savanna, Shane & Kaitlyn back in time to my childhood, because I know they would have loved it. I have so many good memories of camping, and I am hoping the kids look back and have at least one good memory of it. We just got home from camping. We tried really hard, I swear. I think we had a pretty good time, but let me recap a few of the highlights.

Note...we're home a day early.

We packed the truck, completely to the brim, and after it was covered with a blanket, a net, and a tarp, we looked exactly like the "Beverly Hillbillies" and I'm not kidding. All we were missing was the rocking chair on top.

Chad decided to check all the tie downs and bungee cords "one last time" and when he was done, he decided to check them again "one last time." By this point, I was waiting in my car for him to finish and pull the truck out, so I could park my car in the driveway. I watched him tug on every tie down, pat everything down, tuck in the tarp, and then check the bungee cords again "one

117

last time." As he did it, he thought it would be a good idea to stretch the cord as far as it could go, and it was a great idea until it unhooked and came at him like a rocket. It knocked him to the ground and then, before I could pull in, he was in the house. I was terrified that I would see his eyeball on the floor in the laundry room and a trail of blood to the bathroom but, thankfully, the hook caught him above the lip, under the eye and then over the eye, but not in the eye. Immediately, he had a black eye, very swollen, and Stephen fixed the cord.

So, off we went. After multiple bathroom stops (and a stop for sunglasses now that Chad couldn't see) we were off up the hill.

Six people in one completely packed truck for 3 hours, but we finally got there and really, the scenery was beautiful.

That was, until the chipmunks came. I didn't mind, but I'm not sure the camping chair was well equipped to hold a standing seventeen-year-old female who perched herself on it. She finally got used to those, but the spiders, the bugs, the butterflies— that about put her over the edge.

She did, however, manage to go fishing with us, but I am not sure she smiled one time. At all. I am just happy she didn't go fishing again later in the day because, while Chad caught several fish, he didn't realize he was standing in a snake nest and mommy and babies were wrapped around his leg.

Shane, however, learned all sorts of things about survival, including how to whittle wood into spears (I think we have 15 now) and how to make para-cord bracelets (Dawn brought crafts and I am forever indebted to her). Somehow, he convinced Doug (Chad's brother in law) to teach him how to make a "dead fall" – some sort of survival contraption that involved a large, heavy, flat rock held up on sticks and a trap so whatever went under it would get squished. Of course, Savanna was hoping Chip & Dale would run under it.

Very quickly, we realized we forgot the air pump, and after multiple trips to the "lodge" looking for a pump, another air mattress or even a swim raft, Chad realized the lodge had an air compressor. So, back he went to the campsite, got the air mattress, took it back there, hooked it up, and unbeknownst to him and Savanna, the compressor had an oil leak so, as it turned on, oil shot up everywhere and on some other guy's chair (who was staying *there). That guy's $10 chair cost Chad $16 in Budweiser but, by God, we had a full mattress. Which, incidentally, didn't stay full for more than 2 hours.*

However, we finally had dinner and Kaitlyn cooked at least 50 marshmallows, and after everything was put away, we all went down for a "restful" night's sleep. Except, Savanna went to bed crying with her bladder full, because she refused to use the vault toilet and was sure a bear was coming.

We made it through night one, and through the next day with several rounds of "Uno," "Yahtzee," and "Game of Things." That night, we decided spaghetti was a good idea. It was great 'til clean up. Have you ever made spaghetti sauce in the same pot, then used that pot to clean the dishes? Yeah , me

121

neither. Until the other night.

Several Savanna anxiety attacks later, suddenly, she just feels sooo much better, but then it was Kaitlyn's turn to not feel well. At least she threw up at the water pump, then got over it.

This morning, after a big breakfast, we just decided that it was time to come home. So, we packed up our three tents, two coolers, a deflated air mattress, a stove, a table, six chairs, six sleeping bags, fishing poles, three dozen sodas, four bins, six whittled walking sticks, ten para-cord bracelets and prayed we didn't have a stow-away chipmunk or bug in our bag.

We made it home, this time with just tie-downs (no bungee cords), and I've never seen anybody run to a shower so fast. I'm pretty sure if we could have found a hazmat facility where she could have gone through a disinfecting process, she would have done it.

Anyway, all in all, it was pretty fun, but I think next time, Chad and I are going alone, or at least only taking Karl and Cletus...but then again...maybe not.

So, thank you for all YOUR hard work when you guys took us camping. I had NO IDEA being on the parent side of things stunk so bad!

#ithinkshealwaysknewwewereassholes

"Why Can't You Just Unload the Dishwasher?"

I took my family on a field trip once. I told them to get dressed, brush their hair, put on good, firm walking shoes, and gather up whatever they needed to be comfortable. Once I gathered them in the living room, made sure they were all set and ready to go, we embarked on our adventure. Straight to the dishwasher.

For a minute, they were confused. I smiled at their quandary. I had evil, secret thoughts of happiness in my black heart. I could see the look of disgust on their beautiful faces as they slowly put my scheme together in their heads. The clearer it became, their faces changed and their arms folded. I gave them a crooked grin. I probably winked.

My voice dripped with sarcasm as I pointed at the contraption. "This, my loves, is a dishwasher." Doing my best Vanna White impression, I continued. "You see, you can open this door and it just folds right down. You can put dishes inside of it. You can put cups inside of it. You can put silverware inside of it. You can do all of this without barely breaking a sweat." They collectively rolled their eyes. "And then, if there are clean dishes inside, you can just remove those and put them in a cabinet."

My explanation was thorough. In between the heavy sighing and stammering of little feet, it was well received. For a week. I even left out a stack of red plastic cups for their drinking pleasure.

Then, one night, I came home from work. A long, twelve-hour shift. Exhausted, I stumbled into the bedroom, changed from my work pants to my yoga pants and tied my hair into a messy bun. I wanted a hot bath. I wanted some sleep. But, first, a nice glass of wine to take the edge of the day off.

Oh, how I wished at that moment that I actually used my yoga pants for yoga. Oh, how I wished I knew how to do relaxation breathing. The only time I ever learned how to "breathe through" something was when I was in labor and by the time my cervix was opened to a 4, there was no calm breathing, just screaming and f-bombs. This situation was no different.

As I sauntered into the kitchen and saw it, horror music played. You know, the fucking track they use in the movies when some serial killer is stabbing his victim by the lake at summer camp? My eyes fixated on it. The vein in my neck started bulging. My blood pressure shot to unsafe levels.

Seventeen, yes, seventeen cups in the damn sink. Not one. Not five. Seven-fucking-teen. Apparently, my son decided to clean out his room. I am not sure why he loved chocolate milk so much, but I am sure by the looks of it there was a lone cow standing in a field somewhere crying in pain with sore teats from milk depletion. I tried to calm down. I really did. But wasn't it just the week prior I showed the little shits how to put those in the dishwasher?

"Okay," I told myself. "Breathe. Breathe like they showed you in Lamaze." *Hee, hee, ha, ha, ho, ho.* "Maybe the dishwasher is full. Maybe he had to go rescue a baby animal somewhere. Maybe he twisted his arm carrying it all to the sink and he had to go to the emergency room." I flung open the dishwasher. Empty. EMPTY. I screamed.

I-lost-my-shit.

I had had it.

I was done.

I slammed the dishwasher shut. I called out for him. I called out for anybody who would listen. His bedroom door opened, and he ran down the hall.

"What's wrong? What happened? Why are you screaming?" He was worried.

Fire burned in my eyes.

He backed away.

I pointed to the sink.

"Oh yeah, I cleaned out my room."

My   eyes   bulged.
"WHYARETHEDISHESNOTINTHEDISHWASH
ER?" Yes, I said it like it was all one word.

"I dunno."

127

"You DON'T know?" He shrugged his shoulders. He might have smiled. "Alright, that's it. That's IT! I will show you 'I don't know.' You're going to be sorry. I have HAD IT."

I don't even know what he said, if he even said anything. I blew past him and into the garage, grabbing the first storage bin I could find. I wrestled with it while I dragged it through the laundry room and over the heap of towels that somebody left on the floor. By the time I got back to the kitchen, he was gone and in his place was my husband.

"Are you okay, dear?" He quipped.

"No-I-am-not-fucking-okay."

He knew better than to say another word. He watched, silently, while I packed the dishes. He said nothing as I loaded the container with our plates, bowls, cups, silverware. Everything. I packed the mother fucking kitchen.

When I was done, he addressed it. With his eyes wide open, he leaned in and whispered, "What are they supposed to eat off of?"

128

I took three deep, controlled breaths before I turned away and dug out one place setting for each of the children living in my house. One plate, one bowl, one cup, one silverware setting. I surprised myself at how calm I was while I placed the items on the counter. I turned to look at him and paused before I spoke. I cleared my throat.

"There."

I don't remember if it was me or my husband who explained it to the kids. Probably him. I am sure I had blacked out from banging my head on the wall. Nobody said anything as I walked by them and they were cleaning off their one dish when they were hungry again. My son never said anything while he soaked off the milky film from his cup. I'm sure they were terrified. Even my husband must have been scared because, a few days later, I found him standing at the coffee maker pouring coffee into a small, pink, toy teacup he must have found in my daughter's playset.

"What are you doing?" I was puzzled.

"I never got my allotment."

I found the man a coffee cup. In his car. In a cardboard box where he stored them after he took them to work. Twenty-five of them. On occasion, I would find that box on the front porch, like he was leaving me a gift. Well, buddy, you can't have them all, but you can have my "Tinkerbell" coffee cup. I think it eventually became his favorite.

Maybe my youngest daughter was too young to remember this incident, because just today, *yes just today,* she asked me if she could clean the kitchen for money. Wait. You mean you want to clean up your mess and have me pay you? In money? As opposed to giving you a roof over your head and food to eat? Um, no.

My husband was better with the kids. Way more patient. Much more forgiving.

Until that one night.

I don't know why, but when my kids would need to get something out of a cabinet that was mounted on the wall, they would climb up onto the counter, open both cabinet doors and, in an effort to hold themselves up, they would often (and it better have been subconsciously) pull back on the doors to balance themselves. I never thought much about it until, one night, I heard a crash and subsequent screaming.

Oh, for the love of all that's Holy, what now?

I followed the sounds of the screams, pretty confident that nobody was dead since he was still yelling. What I found was my son, on the counter in the laundry room, with all of the contents of what used to be in the cabinet on the floor below him. Art supplies. Glue. Glitter. Paper. Pens. Popsicle sticks. Batteries. A random video game controller. Halloween blood. A ski pass. A bunch of fucking junk I stashed up there. And on top of him, the cabinet, which luckily, when it came down, hit the wall behind him and, thankfully, didn't crush him. Yes, friends, after all those years of hanging on it, it finally came unhinged, pretty much like me. I knew I had to help him although I did quickly calculate how long he might be able to stay in that position, holding up the cabinet, before he fell. I took position under him, held up the cabinet myself so he could get out, and what do you think he did?

He left me there.

So, at that point, I am holding up the cabinet, trying to balance my footing on some old phone book on the ground. I have one free hand. Barely. I manage to reach my cell phone and type out a quick message to my husband, who was at work. As a police officer.

"Need help."

I meant to follow up with something like, "I just need you to lift something." Or, "The cabinet fell, and I can't get it back up." Or, "Just need your help really quick." That would have been great, but as soon as I finished the first text, of course the phone fell on the floor, out of my reach, and there was no way I was letting go of the cabinet to try to get it. And, for some odd reason, nobody came running to help me. But, maybe, that was because in all the commotion, somehow the laundry room door shut, and nobody could hear my muffled screams. My husband never texted me back. After about five minutes, I was sure I was going to meet my untimely death when the cabinet came crashing down on my head. This wasn't the way I wanted to go. No, I had big plans. At least let me be drunk on vodka, dancing in the streets or something. Not this. Not crushed by a cabinet. In the laundry room. My least favorite room.

Just when I was about to give up, I heard it. The garage door opening. Somebody was home. Somebody was going to save me. There was a pause before the back door to the garage opened. It was like whoever was out there was planning something. Come to find out, they were.

Because just then, just as the back door swung open, the front door did as well, and the deep voices of many men came ringing through the house.

"Police! Police!"

You have got to be shitting me.

Yes, folks. I should have finished that text.

When they found me, in the laundry room, holding the cabinet with its contents all over the floor, they couldn't help but laugh. I was in my pajamas. I was tired. I was stuck in pure hell. I didn't even have any make-up on. They patted my husband on the back and wished him well. My husband didn't say a word. Not one word. Not one laugh. Not one sound.

He and his buddy lifted it off. His friend was trying to help without giggling. That was working until the last little bits of glitter came tumbling down on my head when they moved it.

My husband still didn't break a smile. I tried to give him sad, puppy eyes, but still nothing. They carefully placed the cabinet on the floor in the kitchen.

Oh, how I wish I had given him a better coffee cup.

Speaking of coffee cups, it worked. It really did. Because a month after I packed up the kitchen,

I was lying in bed, watching mindless reality shows, when my son came in, sat down, and quietly told me he had a question for me.

"What do I have to do to earn back the forks?"

I composed a list of chores in my head as rainbows appeared in my room and unicorns danced around in delight.

Yes. My work here is done.

Yes, I'm an asshole, too.

By now, you either love me or hate me. Either one is okay. You know what they say, opinions are like assholes and everybody has one. When my husband died, I was given the gift of just not caring anymore what people thought about me, but if I could bring a little joy into their lives, I was going to do it.

In saying that, I am so glad I have the kids I do. They have challenged me, surprised me, impressed me, shocked me, made me laugh, made me cry, and made me angry, but above all, they have shown me what true, unconditional, uninhibited love is. In spite of me, they turned out great. In spite of me, they turned out to be productive, wonderful, beautiful adults. And, most importantly, they have an amazing sense of humor. At least, I hope so.

When my son went to boot camp, I was worried. Not so much about the bombs crashing overhead or the danger of the job. No, I knew he could handle himself. I had, and still have, faith in him. I was worried that the big old military people would be mean to him and yell at him. The first time I was able to talk to him while he was there, I asked him if they yelled at him a lot. He said they did. I asked him if it bothered him. He said it didn't, that after being raised by me, the military was easy. My heart swelled up with pride. He had finally got it. All he had to do was keep his mouth shut and he would be fine.

My older daughter is very successful on a full ride scholarship to a prestigious university. She's going to be the first woman President, I am sure of it. She is a hard worker, she is kind to people, she studies hard and has a witty sense of humor to boot.

My step-son is also in the military, having a successful career and raising a family of his own. And, I'll bet he makes them do their own dishes.

My teenager, well, the jury is still out. But, no matter how much she pushes my buttons right now, I am pretty sure I will really like her when she's about 25 and her frontal lobe is more developed. And, as much as she acts like a fifteen-year-old should act, sometimes, I still see that sweet little girl with her big, beautiful eyes staring up at me begging me to watch her do a somersault. Because it's still there. It's still in there. All that sweetness is still there and, someday, it will all come pouring out again. In the meantime, I am just going to laugh at the stories.

You see, friends, this book is supposed to be funny. It's supposed to tell you silly stories about our crazy life in the hopes that you can laugh and nod your head saying, "That happens at my house, too!"

And if it didn't, and life is cookie cutter perfect for you, and your kids never mess up or give you something to laugh about or stories to tell than, to be honest, I kinda feel bad for you.

Because I would not trade my family for the world. I wouldn't give up the chaos or the craziness or the quips or the challenges, not for one second. Not one.

They make my world go 'round. They make sad days brighter. They make me smile, they make me laugh, and they have given me memories that I will never forget.

And, besides, like I have said before, they've given me really cool stories to tell their kids. And I have the pictures to prove it.

Enjoy your kids. Find the fun. Color. Lay on the driveway and count stars. Scream when you're the passenger and they're learning how to drive. Go into hysterics when you're looking at cars for your kid and, when you're talking about how many miles are on the car, they ask you what happens when they run out of miles. Dance in the kitchen. Tell jokes. Poke fun at each other sometimes. Love them fiercely. But above all, laugh. *Just laugh.*

I couldn't wrap up this book without including the ever popular "Shaneisms" that I posted for years on my Facebook page. You know when kids say something that takes you off guard but they're so funny you can barely stand it? That was my boy. Enjoy!

      1.   Funny text message of the day... me (to Kaitlyn) "You ok?" Kaitlyn's response: "Yes mother. I'm just fine. Are you okay?" Me (a little taken back) "Lol, yes, but I worry about you. Drink some water." Her: "No, water is for the weak. I only drink pure protein mix with 1% milk." Me (now confused) "What?" Long delay...then, "Shane had my phone." Of course, he did.

      2.   Beaming with pride, I said to him "You've had so much good experience lately, riding with the police department and fire department. What a great opportunity to kind of decide what you want to do. What's next?" Him: "I'm riding with the sanitation department next week."

3.   "Mom, I need to have a serious talk. I have a serious question." Me: "What's that?" Him: "How old do you think a highway needs to be before you tell them they're adopted?"

4.   (During an end of the world threat), "Saw a bunch of Mayans at Walmart tonight finishing up their Christmas shopping. They seemed a little rushed."

5.   We were starting to watch "The Backup Plan." Shane asks me what it's about. I read the preview that says, "She gets artificially inseminated and then meets the man of her dreams." Shane then asks me what artificially inseminated means. I immediately have the deer in the headlights look. He sees that and says, "Wait. Are we talking about a turkey baster?"

141

6.   We were talking about the "big brother" program. I asked him if he will ever want to be a big brother. He says, "I dunno if I'll have time with the baby coming in the next couple of months".

7.   In a card to my mother for Mother's Day, he wrote: Thank you for being such a great mom to our mom so she could be a great mom to us!! (Kinda).

8.   I was watching 16 and Pregnant, and Shane asks, "Can't we put something family friendly on?" I retort, "This is family friendly and very educational." Reassuringly, he says, "Mom. I'm not going to get pregnant."

9.   Last night his dad offered to bring him and Savanna a treat and was also

going to bring something for Kaitlyn. I told Shane "Your dad has always liked little kids and been good to them." Not missing the opportunity, Shane says "Is that why you guys got divorced?"

10.   Shane had a friend spend the night the other night who was being a little shy. I asked Shane if his friend was afraid of us. Without missing a beat, he says, "No, but I am."

11.   I was cupping Karl's face, doing the baby talk thing and gave him a kiss. Shane walks by and I kissed Karl again. Shane stops and says, "You know mom, when you kiss him—he's really thinking about me."

12.   We were talking about dog years and kids. Somehow, Kaitlyn came up. I

143

said, "Ya, she's wild. I don't know what's going on with her." Shane: "Hmmm. It could be her friends. Drugs. Alcohol." He leans in to me, "Or discipline issues at home. But, you know, who am I? Just sayin'."

13.   The kids are having a group doctor appointment. After blood pressure checks, weight, height, etc., the doctor starts asking individual questions. He starts with Kaitlyn and asks me "She hasn't started her period yet, right?" (Awkward but I guess he has to ask)...anyway, he then turns to Shane and says, "And, how are you?" Shane says, with a straight face, "Pretty good. I haven't started my period yet either." I almost peed my pants.

14.   My first text abroad to Shane went something like this: Me: "Hi." Him: "Hi." Me: "How are you?" Him: "Good." Me:

"What have you been doing?" Him: "Drugs and partying. Oh, and we don't have a house anymore." Way to put a mom at ease!

15.   Shane and his "big brother" Dylan are being interviewed tomorrow (I think for the IPT) about the Big Brother/Big Sister program in Boise. It's supposed to be in Sunday's paper. And no matter what Shane says, his dad did not die in 9-11 and his mother did not leave him to pursue her crack addiction.

16.   Yesterday, I took out the trash, pulled weeds, and then helped Savanna take her chicken off the bone. Shane slithers up next to me and asks, "Did you lose all your estrogen?"

17.   Just got a call from Shane. "Did everything go okay?" Him: "Yeah, I'm

in the airport." Me: "Have you called Gramma yet?" Him: "No, I met some guy on the plane and I'm just gonna get a ride with him."

18.   OMG. It's already started. Shane, looking concerned, comes up to me and asks, "Did it hurt mom?" As I walk into his trap I respond, "Did what hurt Shane?" Puppy dog eyes followed while he said, "When you fell from Heaven?" Oh, give me a break!

19.   About two days after Savanna left for school, I commented that I missed her. Shane said he missed her, too. I was surprised and said, "Really?" His answer: "Yes. I have no one to talk to about my ever-changing body."

146

20.   Me: "What do you want to do for your graduation?" Him: "Graduate."

And you know what he told me? That, now, as an adult, he can't stand dishes in the sink. Ha!

But it's not just Shane who makes silly comments. Today, as we got in the car, Kaitlyn asks if she can spray my perfume. I asked her, "Why, does it stink in here?" She quickly comes back with, "No, but it's gonna."

Happy Parenting All!

About the Author

Diana Stefano lives a happily chaotic life in Idaho surrounded by the people she loves, a couple of dogs she tolerates and one smuggled in cat. While raising her late husband and a gaggle of kids, she always threatened to write a book about them if they didn't shape up and forewarned them she was taking notes. Apparently, her threats didn't work because now there's a book. When she's not plotting her revenge or writing, she likes long walks to the martini bar, sleeping in, hiding from the dogs and chocolate chip cookies.

Made in the
USA
Monee, IL